Th… ight
ge

by Simon Adorian

THE CAST

Mouse

Ben

Billy

Ravi

Jojo

Sam

Mr Hopkins
the class teacher

Mrs Ross
the leader at Woodlands Camp

Scene 1

At Woodlands Camp. All the class, plus Mr Hopkins, are gathered in a field in front of the tents. Everyone is carrying rucksacks, cases, sleeping bags, pillows and camping equipment. Mrs Ross stands in front of the group. She claps her hands loudly to get everyone quiet.

Mrs Ross *(Loudly)* All right, Story Street Primary, I want everyone to gather round in front of the tents. I need to speak to you all.

The children move over to Mrs Ross. They are all chattering excitedly.

Ben I bet it's really spooky in those woods at night.

Mouse I bet it's really cold in the tent.

Jojo You'll be all right – you've got the best sleeping bag.

Mouse Have you seen the mats we've got to sleep on? They're ever so thin. You can feel all the lumps and bumps in the ground underneath them.

Ravi I thought it was going to be bunk beds. I didn't realise we were going to be sleeping on the ground.

Sam Don't be stupid. That's the whole point of camping.

Mrs Ross Come on, boys and girls, do hurry up now. I haven't got all day.

Scene 1

Sam *(Whispers)* She isn't half bossy.

Mr Hopkins Shhh. I heard that, Sam Summerday.

Sam Sorry, Mr Hopkins.

Mrs Ross Now, everyone should know which tent is theirs. Is that right?

Children Yes, Mrs Ross.

Mrs Ross And I hope you've all noticed that each tent has got a different flag on top. That's important because it helps us to sort out the camp duties. So, for instance, who's got the red flag?

Mouse That's us.

Ben We're the reds.

Mrs Ross That means that you two are collecting the wood for the campfire tonight.

Mouse Great!

Mrs Ross And you're on litter duty.
All the other children laugh.

Mrs Ross Greens.

Ravi That's me and Billy.

Mrs Ross You'll be helping in the kitchen.
More laughter.

Billy I don't mind. All the more food for us.

Ben Are Billy and Ravi in the green tent?

Mouse Yup.

Ben That's not fair. It's bigger than the others. And it's got a porch thing.

Mouse It's called an awning. And anyway, it's so Billy can keep his chair in the tent.

Mr Hopkins *(Sternly)* Ben, be quiet and listen.

Ben Yes, Mr Hopkins.

Mrs Ross *(Loudly)* A few rules and boundaries now. First of all, no one is to go into anyone else's tent. Is that clear?

Children Yes, Mrs Ross.

Mrs Ross When you're playing out in this field, you mustn't go past that fence there. In that direction the line of trees is the boundary. And over there it's the woods. And no going into the woods, except when we take you in there.

Ravi *(Whispering)* Sam's got a teddy tied to her rucksack. Look.

Billy So? Lots of people take them when they go away.

Ravi Do you reckon Mr Hopkins has brought his teddy? *(Giggles)*

Mrs Ross Are you boys listening?

Billy
Ravi } Yes, Mrs Ross.

Mrs Ross What did I just say?

Billy No going into the woods.

Mrs Ross Very well. While you're here, we expect you to keep your tents spotlessly tidy. There'll be a tent inspection every morning before we go out for our activities, with awards for the winners.
Mr Hopkins and I will be the judges.

Mr Hopkins And can I just add one thing – there's to be no food in the tents.

Children *(Moaning)* Awww.

Ben *(Whispering)* I bet Mr Hopkins has got some extra food hidden in *his* tent!

Jojo We were going to have a midnight feast.

Mr Hopkins You don't want animals coming into your tent for a snack, do you?

Sam Wow! Squirrels and hedgehogs and things. I wouldn't mind that.

Billy What about rats and foxes?

Mrs Ross Listen now please, children. As well as the competitions, you're going to learn to work together as a team. That's what Woodlands Camp is all about. Our first activity is going to take place in the woods. We'll meet back here in fifteen minutes once you've sorted your tents out. Mr Hopkins – would you lead the boys off to their tents? And I will take the girls.

Everyone files off carrying their kit.

Mrs Ross *(Loudly)* Hurry up, chop, chop, quick as you can.

Scene 2

Night time. It is very dark and quiet. Sam and Jojo are in their tent. In the background there is a strange squeaking sound.

Jojo *(Urgently)* Sam!

Sam *(Drowsily)* Yeah?

Jojo What's that?

Sam What's what?

Jojo That noise.

Sam I didn't hear any noise.

Jojo Listen.

Silence. Then a few more squeaks.

Jojo There!

Sam A squeaking sound. It's spooky. I don't like it.

Louder squeaking.

Sam It's getting nearer, whatever it is.

Jojo I'm scared. It sounds really creepy.

Sam Shhh. It's right outside the tent.

Billy and Ravi are right outside the girls' tent. Ravi is gently rocking Billy's wheelchair backwards and forwards to make the squeaking sound.

Billy Woooo! This is the ghost of Woodlands Camp. I have come to haunt your tents and strike terror into your hearts.

Sam opens the tent and comes out. Jojo follows.

Sam *(Angrily)* Billy Steel! That is not funny!

Ravi Oh yes it is. And you were well scared too. We heard you in there.

Billy *(Copying Jojo)* "I'm scared. It sounds really creepy."

Jojo OK, so we were a bit frightened. Anyone would be if they heard a noise like that. It's so dark and quiet out there.

Sam You should try it on Mouse and Ben. It'd be great to get them.

Billy Nice idea. Which tent are they in?

Jojo Last tent on the left-hand side.

Billy Are you sure?

Jojo Yes, honest.

Ravi No, it's not. That Mr Hopkins' tent, isn't it?

Jojo Yeah. But it'd be good to see him charging about in his stripy pyjamas.

Billy So, come on, which tent is your brother in? We'll see if we can spook him as well.

Sam It's the third tent in the boys' field. See if you can scare them even more than us.

Billy We'll let you know tomorrow.

Ravi See you.

Billy Shhh.

Exit Billy and Ravi.

Scene 3

The next morning. In the field outside the tents. Billy and Ravi are talking with Mouse and Ben. Sam and Jojo come over to join them.

Sam Well, did you manage to give the boys a fright?

Billy It worked a treat. You should have heard Ben – he was totally petrified.

Ben Was not.

Ravi Were too – and you know it. You lot were even more scared than the girls. At least they dared come out of the tent to find out what the noise was. You and Mouse just hid.

Mouse We were just being sensible. For all we knew it could have been something really dangerous out there.

Ben Anyway, we weren't that scared.

Sam Huh! Doesn't sound that way to me.

Ben All right, then, we'll have to find out who's really the bravest.

Jojo How can we do that?

Ben We'll need to set some kind of dare. At night time.

Sam A midnight challenge!

Mouse *(Unsure)* Like what, exactly?

Sam I don't know. Something that proves once and for all who's the braver – you boys or us girls.

Jojo Billy and Ravi should set the challenge if it's going to be fair.

Billy ***(Thinking hard)*** All right, then. Let me think.

Ravi Something really, really daring.

Billy How about this? Go into the woods at midnight. And whichever pair goes the further is the bravest.

Ben That's good.

Scene 3

Jojo One problem. How will we know who's gone further?

Ravi ***(Suddenly excited)*** I know. The flags.

Mouse Eh?

Ravi You have to take your tent flag. So Jojo and Sam take the blue flag, and you and Ben take the red one. And you've got to plant it or hang it in the woods. And whichever flag is the longest way away from here, their tent wins the challenge.

Sam That's brilliant! We're up for it. What about you boys?

Ben All right, then. Count us in.

Sam And the prize?

Billy The losing tent has to do the other tent's duties for the next day.

Sam It's a deal.

Mouse
Jojo
Ben } Deal.

Billy Shake on it.

They all shake hands.

Enter Mrs Ross.

Scene 3

Mrs Ross Any minute now Mr Hopkins will announce the winners of the tent inspections.

Billy Hah! I bet that'll be us.

Mrs Ross I don't think so, Billy Steel. Your tent is the worst of all. Rucksacks tipped out, clothes all over the place. It's a terrible mess.

Scene 3

Billy But ... but ...

Ravi But we spent ages tidying it. It was perfect.

Mrs Ross Nonsense. You're just very untidy boys. Now go back and get it neat and shipshape.

Billy
Ravi } Yes, Miss.

Mrs Ross leads Billy and Ravi back to their tent.

Mouse I don't get it. I saw their tent just now and it was perfect.

Sam Perhaps someone crept in there and messed it up for them.

Scene 3

Jojo *(Mischievously)* Now who would go and do a naughty thing like that, Samantha?

Sam *(Smiling)* I can't imagine, Joanna. Unless it was someone trying to get their own back.

Jojo Tut, tut. What a dreadful thing to do. I'm quite shocked.

Sam Come on. Let's get back to our tent – our very tidy tent.

Exit Jojo and Sam, laughing.

Mouse It was them! They messed up Billy's tent.

Ben Don't worry, we'll get our own back tonight. We're going to win this midnight challenge – you just wait and see!

Scene 3

Scene 4

Night time. In the woods. Sam and Jojo are creeping nervously along a path. Sam is carrying a torch. Jojo is holding a blue flag. They are both talking in whispers.

Jojo Shhh. What was that?

Sam It might have been an animal.

Jojo Turn the torch off. We don't want anyone seeing us.
Sam turns off the torch.

Jojo It's ever so dark, Sam.

Sam Don't worry. We'll get used to it after a bit. We'll just have to walk very slowly. Careful where you tread.

Sam and Jojo move forward very slowly, their hands stretched out ahead of them to feel their way.

Jojo Sam?

Sam Yeah?

Jojo Are you scared?

Scene 4

Sam Course not. We're not going to meet anyone, are we? Just go on for bit longer and plant our flag. Then we'll turn back and head for the camp.

Jojo suddenly slips and there is a small splash.

Jojo Help!

Sam What's up?

Jojo I'm soaked. It must be a little stream. Help me up. Can you turn the torch on for a minute?

Sam fumbles for the torch and drops it.

Sam It won't work. I dropped it in the water and now it won't work.

Sam pulls Jojo up by the hand.

Sam There you go. Are you all right now?

Jojo I'm wet through. I bet I'm covered in mud.

Sam Never mind. It'll wash off. We'll just have to go into the shower block when we get back.

Jojo Do you think Ben and Mouse'll dare to come this far into the woods?

Sam Huh! Doubt it. I expect they're safely tucked up in their sleeping bags.

Sam and Jojo 'freeze'. The action shifts to a nearby part of the woods. Ben and Mouse are carefully picking their way through the trees. Mouse is carrying a red flag.

Mouse Can't we just hang the flag up now, Ben? We must have come miles.

Ben Let's go on a little bit further. We've got to make sure we beat those girls. They'll never let us forget it if they win. You know what Sam and Jojo are like.

Mouse I'd never hear the end of it at home. I guess we'd better go a bit further and ... ***(tripping up)*** ... Woah!

Ben What happened?

Mouse Something tripped me up. I've bashed my knee. Ow. Give me a hand.

Ben goes to help and trips up too.

Ben Hey! What was that?

Mouse I think it must have been this tree root. Are you OK?

Ben Yeah, I'm fine. Just a bit of a bruise. Let's press on.

Scene 4

Mouse Which way?

Ben Keep going straight ahead. The camp's behind us. I can see the lights. Oh no!

Mouse What's up?

Ben My foot's stuck! I've stepped in some kind of a bog. I'm right up to my knee in mud. Help pull me out.

Mouse grabs hold of Ben's arm to pull.

Ben Yeeurghh! It's all squelchy! Watch out you don't tread in this stuff.

Mouse Too late! It's like a swamp. Let me pull you out. I'll hang on to this tree. What a state we're in.

Ben My jeans are filthy. I hope Mr Hopkins doesn't ask any tricky questions tomorrow.

Mouse He probably won't even notice.

Ben Huh, you know what Hoppo is like. He doesn't miss a thing.

Mouse Just tell him it happened when we went on the hike with Mrs Ross. He won't know.

Ben I wish we'd brought a torch with us.

Ben and Mouse 'freeze' as the action shifts back to Sam and Jojo.

Jojo I really think we should turn back now, Sam. I'm freezing and it feels like we've been out here for hours. I'm not even sure which way takes us back to camp.

Sam I'm pretty sure I can get us back. Here, give me the flag.

Jojo hands Sam the blue flag.

Sam I'll just stick it here by this branch.

Sam fixes the flag in a tree.

Sam There. That'll show them who dared go further into the woods. The winners! Yesss!

Sam punches the air and does a little victory dance. As she does this, she trips and falls awkwardly.

Sam Aarggh! My ankle! Help me, Jojo.

Jojo You shouldn't have been leaping around like that in the pitch dark, you twit! Come on, up you get. You'll be all right.

Sam No. It really hurts. It feels like I've broken it. I can't ... I can't stand up. Ow!

Jojo Well, I won't be able to carry you all the way back, will I? There's only one thing for it.

Sam What's that?

Jojo I'll have to go back to camp for help.

Sam Oh no! Think of the trouble we'll get into. Hopkins will go mad!

Jojo But I can't leave you lying here all night, can I?

There is a rustling in the bushes.

Sam *(Whispers)* Shhh. Listen.

Jojo What?

Sam Someone's coming.

Jojo What shall we do?

Sam Just lie very still. Don't move a muscle.

Ben and Mouse approach. They are very nervous and tread carefully. As Ben creeps along, he brushes past Jojo who cries out.

Jojo *(Shouts)* Help!

Ben, Mouse and Sam are all startled and they all jump and cry out.

Mouse Yikes!

Ben Aaah!

Sam Who's that?

Ben It's Sam!

Sam Ben! Mouse! What're you doing here?

Ben What do you think we're doing? Having a picnic? What about you?

Jojo This is as far as we're going. Anyway, it's an emergency. Sam's injured and she can't walk. It's her ankle. We're going to need your help to carry her back to camp.

Mouse OK. We were going to turn round now anyway.

Ben What shall we do with the flag?

Jojo You could put it here next to ours and call it a draw.

Ben What's the point of that?

Jojo Just to prove to Billy, Ravi and the rest that we didn't chicken out. Show them how far we went.

Scene 4

Ben All right.

Mouse hands over the red flag to Ben who plants it next to the blue one.

Sam *(Groaning)* My ankle. It's agony.

Jojo We haven't forgotten you. Right, let's get her up carefully.

Jojo, Mouse and Ben work together to lift Sam and carry her towards the camp.

Ben There we go. Gently does it.

Sam Owww!

Mouse Cor, you weigh a ton.

Jojo *(Sternly)* Mouse!

Mouse Well she does.

Jojo Just get on with carrying her. Which way do we go?

Ben To our left. Just turn her round a bit. That's it. Careful.

Sam Ow – watch what you're doing!

Ben Sorry. We're doing our best.

Jojo You'll be all right when we get back to camp, Sam. Just think what all the others will say when they hear about our midnight adventure.

They slowly make their way back towards the camp.

Scene 5

The next morning. In the field outside the tents. Billy, Ravi, Mouse and Ben are talking together.

Ravi So it was a draw, was it?

Ben That's right.

Billy I reckon none of you even dared go into the woods, so you just made up the whole story.

Mouse No, it's true, honestly. It must have been a five-mile hike at least. We'll see if we can find the flags later. Ask the girls if you want.

Sam and Jojo come over. Sam is limping heavily.

Ben You all right, Sam?

Sam It's ever so sore, but not as bad as I thought. I'll be OK.

Mouse We've told Billy and Ravi a bit about last night. How we went for miles in the pitch dark, trekking into the heart of the woods.

Jojo And how I nearly drowned in a gigantic river …

Mouse And how Ben and me got caught in a lethal mantrap …

Ben And then I was up to my neck in quicksand …

Sam And then I nearly broke my ankle.

Mouse It certainly was an adventure, we can tell you.

Billy and Ravi look impressed.

Billy River?

Ravi Mantrap? Quicksand?

Jojo Yeah! It was tough going but somehow we survived.

Mrs Ross comes across the field carrying the red and blue flags.

Mrs Ross Ah, there you are. Aren't these the flags from your tents?

The children keep silent and look embarrassed.

Mrs Ross Well?

Ben They do look like our flags.

Mrs Ross Perhaps you'd be so kind as to put them back. I've just been in the woods with a group to pick firewood and one of the children found them up a tree. I can't understand it at all.

Billy Where were they, Mrs Ross?

Mrs Ross Over there. Just inside the woods. Only a couple of hundred metres from the camp. Anyway, at least we've got them back. Now let's see how breakfast is coming along.

Mrs Ross walks off quickly.

Billy So it was a five-mile hike, was it?

Sam Only a couple of hundred metres? But it seemed like miles.

Billy *(Laughing)* Don't forget the wide river – and the mantraps!

Ravi And the quicksand!

Mouse At least we weren't scared to take the challenge.

Jojo It was an adventure I'll never forget.

Ben Me neither.

Sam Our midnight adventure!